Velvet STEEL

Other Books by John Piper

Velvet Steel

The Joy of Being Married to You

Selections from the Poems of

JOHN PIPER

CROSSWAY BOOKS

WHEATON, ILLINOIS

Velvet Steel

Copyright © 2009 by Desiring God Foundation

Published by Crossway Books
          a publishing ministry of Good News Publishers
          1300 Crescent Street
          Wheaton, Illinois 60187

Cover design: Josh Dennis

First printing, 2009

Printed in the United States of America

ISBN PDF: 978-1-4335-1132-5

ISBN Mobipocket: 978-1-4335-1133-2

Library of Congress Cataloging-in-Publication Data
Piper, John, 1946–
  Velvet steel : the joy of being married to you : selections from the
poems of John Piper.
    p. cm.
  ISBN 978-1-4335-1131-8
  1. Marriage—Poetry. I. Title.
PR3566.I59V45   2009
811'.54—dc22   2008048761

LB			19	18	17	16	15	14	13	12	11	10	09
15	14	13	12	11	10	9	8	7	6	5	4	3	2	1

To Noël

CONTENTS

Introduction

*T*his poetry is an overflow of my affection for my wife of more than forty years. Two of them are exceptions—they were written by Noël.

Most of them are excerpts from longer poems. The reasons for not including the whole poems is that some are too long and my aim is to give tastes, not meals—tastes of one man's affections for his wife.

I put this collection together in the days immediately after writing a book on marriage called *This Momentary Marriage: A Parable of Permanence.* This collection of poems completes that book. What seemed to be missing there was the taste of my affections for Noël.

In fact, the point of that book was that covenant-keeping, not the affections of being "in love," is the main point of marriage. But I also emphasized that tough-minded covenant-keeping is the best soil for the long-term flourishing of tender affections. Therefore, it seemed helpful that I give some tastes of what those affections were like over the last forty-two years.

Why poetry? Because poetry helps me intensify and express feelings that cannot be captured sufficiently in ordinary language. In fact, my definition of poetry is: *an effort to share a moving experience by using language that is chosen and structured differently from ordinary prose.*

Being in love is a very moving experience. It is like a river that over the years has rushing currents, crashing waterfalls, deep peaceful flows, eddies that swirl with scum, windblown backward drifts, surface heavings from boulders beneath, and long clean stretches of open water.

Not even poetry can render this reality in another form. But some of us must try. It is built into us humans that we must try to express the affections of love in ways that are not like the affections themselves.

We do it with songs, paintings, sculpture, drama, novels, woodwork, flower arrangements, purchased roses, notes left on the dresser, eating out, bed-and-breakfast weekends, repairing the leaky faucet, dressing up, sexual favors, special gifts, surprise phone calls, visiting concerts, movies, museums, gardens, oceans, mountains, and a hundred other ways.

My prayer is that these small tastes of my imperfect affections will fan affections into flame—for God, for your spouse, and, in every fitting way, for all the treasured people in your life.

Marriage is a parable of something greater than itself—the covenant-keeping relationship between Christ and his church. Christ's love for his church was tough enough to keep him on the cross until our purchase was finished.

But it was also tender and warm. Already through the Old Testament prophet, God gave this expression of affection:

> *How can I give you up, O Ephraim?*
> *How can I hand you over, O Israel? . . .*
> *My heart recoils within me;*
> *My compassion grows warm and tender.*
>
> (Hosea 11:8)

May God cause such tender shoots of affection to grow in the covenant-keeping soil of your life. May the fullness of Christ's love be known and shown in the wholeness of every marriage bond.

John Piper

To Come and Capture Me

My love for you, Noël,
will drive me to pursue
with God and you
the one pure love and unity
that God's own Son
did show in birth and death for us.
As He cast off His glory once
to capture me,
so would I shed my freedom now
to gain
Noël.

TO A DIAMOND ON OUR ENGAGEMENT

Dim shadows of a brighter heart:
    These nervous specks of color,
        This little world of light;
            These minute brilliances.

Yet they can sing!
    So sing to her,
        You little brilliances,
            You timid colors,
                You twinkling cosmos.

Sing to her!
    Of God and Heaven,
        Of life and Hope.

Sing to her!
    Of high thoughts,
        Of heart's capacities
        Beyond your own crystal
            realities.

Sing to her!
    Of love
        Of being loved
        With Love more lucid than
            yourself.

And purely sing,
    My little shadows,
And purely sing
    Of me.

A WHISPERED YES

Stunning sometimes to ponder
that all my future knowing
and all my future doing
will be a knowing-with and doing-for;
that you love me enough,
and love me yet,
to whisper me a Yes with your life.

She Kneeled to Be His Wife

Strength comes in all colors
even pink and purple.

I have seen Strength lie down—
like a bulldozer.
I have seen her walk behind—
with the checkered flag.

She has given way to a feather's weight
and lifted mountains with ease.

Strength is a mystery creature
a man might give her his life.
For one, before he could reach her,
she kneeled to be his wife.

THE CHRISTIAN HEDONIST
TAKES A WIFE

Our God has made another way
To put his glory on display.
His goodness shines with brightest rays
When we delight in all his ways.
His glory overflows its rim
When we are satisfied in him.
His radiance will fill the earth
When people revel in his worth.
The beauty of God's holy fire
Burns brightest in the heart's desire.

I am a Christian Hedonist
Because I know that if I kissed
My wife simply because it's right,
And not because it's my delight,
It would not honor her so well.
With pleasures I will praise Noël,
And I will magnify my wife
By making her my joy in life.

So may this blazing, God-like flame
Ignite in us for his great name
A holy passion, zeal and fire
That magnify Him with desire.
I hail Him as my joy in life,
And take from his pure hand my wife.

HEARTBEAT THE MORNING
OF OUR MARRIAGE

Can I despise or doubt his wisdom
who, for ten thousand years,
has made of mortal men
bold conquerors of crisis,
who, from raw human trembling,
has forged finished victories?
Let him rage.
The sound of timid men fades like an echo;
only his thundering rings in history's ears.

Our Wedding Text
Habakkuk 3

Although the fig tree blossom not,
And all the vines of our small plot
Be barren, and the olive fail,
The sheep grow weak and heifers frail,
We will rejoice in God, my love,
And takes our pleasures from above:
The Lord, our God, shall be our strength
And give us life, whatever length
On earth he please, and make our feet
Like mountain deer, to rise and cleat
The narrow path for man and wife
That rises steep and leads to life.

A PROMISE TO BE KEPT

Exquisite incompleteness
disturbs my senses—
There is a joyful promise
to be kept.

Good Promises

Such a prize we have,
and many others,
from the mouth of God.
This grace we get
for nothing we have done,
save not to shun
its worth and grasp at other things.

And this
we give: good promises
to make our flesh as one,
And seal the beauty now,
and future
bliss.

OUR SOLSTICE ANNIVERSARY
DECEMBER 21

How could the universe ignore
Us two becoming one,
As though no strange and awe-full thing
Had happened in the solar ring?

It couldn't. So the plan was laid
By God that notice should be made
Each year on planet earth below
That we are still in love. And so,
To celebrate what we have built,
The planet earth does cease to tilt.

LOVE'S PROMINENCE

Our love is like an upward glance
on a freezing February night:
the moon so dominant as to make
her speckled backdrop blur beyond her
      light,
and no clouds curtaining its prominence
among the universal dance.

EPHESIAN COVENANT

This day's unfit for such a bright affair,
yet it portends for us a happy truth;
for as against its dimness we can shine
with smiles and gleaming eyes and bursting
      hearts,
so also, when these winds shall blow black
      clouds
of grief and pain and sin across our lives,
shall we, by our Ephesian Covenant,
an unextinguished light to our world be.

Nature and Your Face

Since mountains are the weight
and seas the depth
and sky the breadth
of what I feel for you,
may I be never long
apart from Nature or your face.

LOVE NEVER FELT BEFORE

When your eyes began to moisten,
And your throat closed on your voice,
And your breathing came more quickly,
And your body showed your sorrow;

When the room was filled with silence,
And you said that you were sorry,
I loved you with a longing
That I'd never felt before.

JOHN PIPER

Being a Gift on Your Birthday

And the gladness still keeps running down:
one of those endless fountains
that flows for two people who love like
      this.
And, my, doesn't it always taste right!
Like 100-proof patience and gentleness and
      strength.
There is no better flavor than your love.
But then of course I shouldn't doubt the
      Lord's good taste.
How does it feel to be a gift on your own
      birthday?

FEELING A FAKE KISS

Your hair is so much longer now.
I can remember when your neck
was unguarded and I could
make chills run down your
back and goose-bumps pop
out all over—with a fake of a kiss.

HER LOVE, MY DAY AND NIGHT

She is Dawn, new and full of much delight,
Chasing stars, red in the face, she nears,
Flinging colors at the fleeing night,
Flying gold and silver banners, she appears.

She is misty Evening in a green field
Of moist and unmown grass, slowly seeping
From the willows which already lie
      concealed,
Bearing healing from the trees to the
      weeping.

She is the balm of Midnight which one feels;
She blows upon the day's hot wounds and
      scars,
And, as a way of healing, she reveals
The endless sky of galaxies and stars.

DESIGN

If sunshine
Is a happy sign
That the divine
Is oft benign
And can design
A living shrine
And us refine
And so align
That what is mine
Is also thine,

Then you will surely not decline
To be my only Valentine.

Away

Reading in rocking chair,
Butterflies and black bear,

Moss and mushrooms,
Pictures and poems,

Songs and swing,
Woodpeckers on wing,

Worship and walking,
Time for talking,

Scrabble and sleep . . .
A quiet to keep.

BY NOËL

A TENDER PIECE OF SOVEREIGNTY

It was a loving Providence and wise,
Who did the union of our lives devise;
A tender piece of sovereignty
Behind and in our fortune lies.

Wo Brennt die Liebe Immer Fort

Erfahren habe ich mit dir
All dieses Glück und vielles noch;
Und, dass du immer warst bei mir,
Verdoppelt all mein Freude, doch!

Nun wohnen wir am kalten Ort,
Doch bleibt die Liebe immer warm.
Wo brennt die Liebe immer fort,
Da macht die Kälte keinen Harm.

Ich will zum Schluss Gebet aufheben:
Die Freude dieses ein Jahrzehnt—
Mög' das begleiten uns durchs Leben,
Und dann auf ewig ausgedehnt.

Georgia Belle

God bless you southern lady fair
Best wishes Georgia Belle.
The pine scent lingers in your hair,
I love you, dear Noël.

"JUST TELL ME WHEN TO PACK"

But when I called to you that night,
And said, "Noël, I think I might
Just sell the house and car and go
To some far distant land to sow
The gospel where no one has gone
And make the light of Jesus dawn,"
Your voice unwavering came back,
And said, "Just tell me when to pack."

PITY MILLIONAIRES

Sun falls and God sets out his flares.
Come now, and sit with me, my wife,
And let us pity millionaires,
And savor every breath of life.

Paradise Still Cursed

Our sixteenth year has been the best and
　　worst:
Lest too much paradise become uncursed;
The enemy has sown his kudzu vine
Across the dogwood and the mountain pine
To wrap the blossom and the wood in gloom
And make the bower of our love a tomb.

Yet petals of the dogwood hold their scent,
And kudzu presses down but can't prevent
The pow'rful pine from pushing into light.
The roots are deep; a river runs at night
And holy angels with machetes slash
The evil vines and turn them into ash,
And spread them out to fertilize the earth
And give the garden of our love new birth.

NONE BUT YOU

Whose tears have soaked my collar dark?
    None but yours, no, none but yours.
Whose sorrows leave the deepest mark?
    None but yours, no, none but yours.

Who gave herself to me alone?
    None but you, no, none but you.
Who is the only one I've known?
    None but you, no, none but you.

There is no other I desire,
    None but you, no, none but you.
Till death my deepest friend, my fire:
    None but you, no, none but you.

The Way to Joy

> "The way of man
> Lies not within himself." And what then can
> He do but plan his way and watch the Lord
> With all his knowing love—for me . . . and
>   you,
> And for the priceless sons that he foreknew.
> So let us be at peace within our lot,
> God knows the way to joy when we do not.

How Firm You Deal

For eighteen years I've marveled now,
How free and firm you deal,
Therefore, I thank the Lord and bow
Before your velvet steel.

ROOTS

I bless the Lord for Henry roots
That I have come to know,
And for the firstborn of their shoots
Now forty years ago.

I bless him for the branch begun
And nourished from their stock,
And for your angle in the Sun,
And nurture in the Rock.

I bless him for the wind that blew
And brought you second life,
And for the grace that made you new,
And then made you my wife.

I bless him for the steady course
And for the even keel,
For solid bone along your back,
And for the velvet steel.

THE FEEBLE RICH

May stars at night and blue-gold morning
    light
point us to riches high
and sure, if we should live or die.
Did not he pay his all, that we,
my bright

    companion, be the feeble rich who see
    the greater wealth of joy
    and love, and all our life employ
    to spread this humble wealth and make
    it free.

Valentine's Grace

It's only fit that in our little span
Of married life the good and secret plan
That governs all our feasts and Valentines
Should order some to be blue sky that shines
And others gray and even ominous:
Both serve our love, and sweetly couple us.

THiS MARRiAGE:
OLD OR YOUNG?

At twenty-four is marriage old
    or it is young?
I think the answer comes to this:
Have all the songs been sung?

Have all the songs been sung,
    or are there any more?
I think the answer comes to this:
Can aging poets soar?

Can aging poets soar,
    or are the wings too weak?
I think the answer comes like this:
Is all the beauty bleak?

Is all the beauty bleak,
    and nothing left but pain?
I think the answer comes to this:
Does any love remain?

Does any love remain,
    or has it turned to stone?
I think the answer comes like this:
Is God still on the throne?

GOING FOR GOLD

What a way to prepare for our party—
was it you who hurt me or I you?
But our smiles were constrained to seem
      hearty—
a veneer we were all too used to.

"May the next twenty-five be as great as
the first!" they said with their hugs and
      smiles,
While I tried to dream up an alias
I'd adopt after bolting for miles.

But I knew I would stay. How could I flee
the one who knew me, yet loved me still?
Then Beryl, whose years with Arnold were
      sixty,
matter-of-factly thawed my heart's chill.

"The years that are coming will be the best;
"The first twenty-five are the hardest."

BY NOËL

Go Make a Parable
for Jesus' Sake

In spite of all
My sin, God said, "Now go, enthrall
Yourself with her, and call her your
Delight, and keep your love as pure
As mine for you. She is a gift
From me. And if you ever lift
Your hand or voice against your wife,
Remember that I hold your life
Here in my hand. Instead, go make
A parable for Jesus' sake,
And show the world the kind of grace
That put Noël in your embrace."

I fear I have not written well
This parable, and truth will tell
How marred the tender tablets are,
And time will show how deep the scar
That I have left with my poor script.
Too seldom was my stylus dipped
In oil before I wrote in this

Velvet STEEL

Soft clay. Some things a tender kiss,
Cannot undo, and worse is none
Than this: The good that was not done.
The happy praises left unsung,
The bell of thankfulness unrung,
The exultation left unsaid,
And tears of sympathy unshed.

I wish that I could start again.
But that is not to be. So then,
I will make good on this our day
Of anniversary, and say,
My wife is to be praised! Let this
Be sung today. Nor will I miss
This chance to ring the happy bell
Of hope and thankfulness, and tell
The world in words, I can't conceal
The exultation that I feel,
And inasmuch as it lies in
My pow'r, to let the tears begin.

God has been good to me. Far more
Than I deserve he put in store,
And made me drink the cup of bliss
From your kind hands, and taste the kiss
Of mercy all these solid years,
In spite of all my sin. No fears
Destroy my hope that we will last,
Because God's mercy is steadfast,
And he delights to cross the broad
Expanse of all my sin, my flawed
Creation of this parable
Of love, and by his nearness, full
Of truth, make marriage here a place
To write the story of his grace.

AND RIPENED FULL,
FED HER BELOVED

A good wife he has found from solid stock,
whose flame was bright and warm when she
> *first loved,*
and then, burned brighter with the years;
> *and whose*
first fruit was dripping-sweet and, ripened
> *full,*
fed her beloved all that he could use.

A Season That Will Pass

When God is over all the year,
White snow and virgin grass,
We know that ice will disappear,
And winter soon will pass.

When God is over all the year,
And lakes are crystal brass,
We know the melting too is near,
And frozen spring will pass.

When God is over all the year,
And trees are dipped in glass,
Each twig will shed its April tear,
And icy wind will pass.

When God is over all the year,
And March is dark, alas!
We know that dismal skies will clear,
And darkness too will pass.

When God is over all the year,
And wintry days harass,
We need not dread nor need we fear
A season that will pass.

A CRYSTAL TEAR

Is
this a
crystal tear
that I could kiss
away with some soft
word of whispered sorrow
pressed with penitential lips
upon the wounded spot beneath
your breast? Or did it fall this far because
you smiled, and made your cheek rise rounded
underneath your glistening eye? Let both or
either one be true, I fear and hope that I
have made it fall, and hope and fear
that I may kiss, yet far too oft
to heal, and not enough
to make you
smile.

To Look at All Things New

Who would have thought that you and I,
At almost fifty years,
Would precedent and plan defy,
And alter our careers?

Who would have thought at this late date
That we would have the right
To cherish and to incubate
Our little Moabite.

But twenty-seven years of trust,
And twenty-three with boys,
Has taught us well how to adjust
And where to find our joys.

And so I enter twenty-eight
With Talitha and you.
And know that it is not too late
To look at all things new.

HOSEA AND GOMER

And when they looked into
Each other's eyes, as they would do
At night, they knew, as none could know
But they, that God would bend his bow
Against the charms of foreign men,
And take his faithless wife again.
They knew it could and would be done,
As surely as the rising sun
Drives darkness back unerringly,
And drowns it in the western sea.
They knew, because they had rehearsed
The tragedy and played it first
Themselves with passion and deceit.

Hosea loved beyond the way
Of mortal man. What man would say,
"Love grows more strong when it must wait,
And deeper when it's almost hate."

"And children," Gomer said with tears,
"Mark this, the miracle of years."
She looked Hosea in the face

And said, "Hosea, man of grace,
Dark harlotry was in my blood,
Until your love became a flood
Cascading over my crude life
And kept me as your only wife.
I love the very ground you trod,
And most of all I love your God."

THE GADARENE IN HIS RIGHT MIND

"How many years apart
Have I lived from my wife and son?"
"Near seven years. But, Alex none,
Not even one, did she forsake
Her covenant. Nor did she make
The slightest overture to men.
I think she'd like to see you when
You have the strength to go."

RUTH

"Besides this well-taught speech, reveal
Your own designs, and how you feel
Tonight about Naomi's mind.
Or have you no emotions unassigned?"
She lay there motionless, then said,
"My heart's desire is that you spread
Your holy wing and cover me."

BOAZ

He took his shoe and gave it to
Me in the gate. I turned and threw
It out to Ruth among the crowd.
She caught it like a wreath, and bowed.
I quieted the shouts and cried,
"What do you think of this my bride?"
And she replied, "I think the Lord
Has fought today, and with his sword
Has stuck a sign up on the gate
And hung on it our wedding date.
As for the badge of shame, you tell:
The line of Judah bears it well,
And will for generations yet
To come."

JOB

　　　　　And Dinah sobbed.
And tears ran down Job's horrid face.
He pulled himself up from his place,
And by some power of grace, he stood
Beside his wife and said, "I would,
No doubt, in your place feel the same.
But, wife, I cannot curse the name
That never treated me unfair,
And just this day has answered prayer."
"What prayer? What did you bid him do?"
"That I should bear this pain, not you."

These were his thoughts as they embraced,
Who knows how long. (There is no haste
In grief.) "Job." "Yes, Dinah?" "You know,
It was a long, long time ago
That you held me this way—so long
And tight, and without sex, and strong.
I might survive if you would stay
And hold me like this every day."

DAWN
ON HEARING THAT I HAVE CANCER

*As we look up the western steeps
That make this path a valley where
We walk on solid stone, there leaps
Sure-footed like a mountain flare
This golden edge, this line of light,
All jagged on a wall of stone,
Down, down with every crag as bright
Above the line as if there shone
A mount of fire spreading down
These cliffs to clothe the valley here
With one enfolding golden gown
Of light until the sun appear
Above the dismal eastern rim
And blast, as in the twinkling of
An eye, the final scraps of dim
And gloomy ground with gleaming love,
And banish every shadow in
This world.*

That Fragile Afternoon

What does
The winter mean to us! Another ring
Of solid wood, another ripening
With flow'rs and fruit and feasting in the sun,
Pressed down, solidified, beneath a ton
Of snow, until the fibers form like steel,
Another thick unbending ring and seal
Of how I feel for you now forty years
Since that first fragile afternoon.

THAT GLAD AFTERNOON
WHEN WE FIRST MET

> *This is a tree*
With forty rings of love, all thick with joy,
Made firm with winter sorrows that destroy
Frail flowers, but for us encircle spring
And summer bliss, and make another ring
Of solid love. I bless you, happy June
> *Of sixty-six, and that glad afternoon.*

THE SERVANT OF OUR LOVE

Cold winds can cut not only through
Thick coats, and make a person blue,
But also, like a blade of ice,
Can sever one in two, and slice
A wisely interwoven whole
In twain, as if a single soul,
Alone in pain, were somehow more
To be desired, and this at war,
Than one sweet woven life from two,
And union deep, like me and you.

Or icy wind, with razor's edge,
That threatens to become a wedge,
And put asunder what the Lord
Has made, can fail; and such a sword
Become the common foe that drives
Two beaten souls and threatened lives
Together in the icy blast.
And is this not our lot at last?
Cold winds are ruled by powers above,
And made the servant of our love.

YOUR MIRRORED TREASURES SHINE

A treasure five times over are
You now. Four sons, each one
A precious stone to me, and far
More that, when each is done

Delighting in his mother's life,
And making thus a treasure out
Of you, and adding worth to wife
And friend and my own flesh. I doubt

That there are instruments for this:
To measure mirroring of worth
In worth, of wife in son. One kiss
Can capture more of this, and birth

More measurements of mirrored love
Than any scale or mere device
On earth. Its origin above
Brooks no control or measured price.

And now another precious stone
Hangs 'round your neck, a girl, alone
And beautiful among these sons,
And in her precious eyes and mine
Again your mirrored treasures shine.

TRUST HIM WHO CUTS

If I am like a bow bent tight
With hope, and strung with prayer,
And you my quiver, and the might
To bend me more and bear
With me the tautness of our bow,
Then may we not, good mate,
Trust him who cuts and carves, to grow
The arrows of our quiver straight?

LEANING INTO YOU

I used to dream about becoming old,
And leaning on your heart so long I'd fold
It into mine, like that old hickory tree
Along the cottage path, that after three,
Or four, or maybe five decades, has pressed
Itself against the fencing wire with rest
Unceasing, till, without a drop of blood,
The pith is pierced, and every barb a bud.

Now, barely shy of half a century,
And long since pierced with fierce fidelity,
I dream about becoming older still,
And how some day beside the Brightwood
      mill,
Between the watercourse and stream, four
      sons
And faithful wives, and all their little ones,
Will rise and bless the velvet steel where I,
And they, have leaned, and will until we die.

A Mother's Day Vision

The city is gone
wrapped in a rose haze
predawn
garments of the last days
when Babylon will be no more
and I will stand
after the war
on a slope in Hillside
near an empty grave
and take your hand
unwifed
but not unloved
and we shall go
to visit cities
where our sons
risen
rule over ten.

On Becoming a Grandmother

Who's the lady here beside me
    sound asleep without a care?
Who's the lady breathing slowly
    with the soft and flowing hair?

She's the woman that I married
    on a day when heaven smiled,
And the mother of the father
    of my son's first child.

BRAIDING TALITHA'S HAIR

Stand there behind your little girl today,
And mark the year that you were born in this
Dark winter month, and let your fingers say
With tenderness and skill how sweet the
    bliss

Of tending this dark hair, as if a kiss
Were put with finger-lips on each fine braid.
And from the depths of womanhood dismiss
Through this dear touch from you the
    treasure laid

In your young soul with finger-kisses made
From other women gone before, who wove
Their womanhood into your life, and paid
Their precious portion to your mother-trove.

Weave treasures now into this child. Make
    good
Your work and waken here new
    womanhood.

LOSSES
ON TURNING SIXTY

Toward sixty, losses multiply.
The pace and pain we cannot stop:
How suddenly the petals dry,
And as if in agreement, drop.

And sometimes even little buds
Are lost, cut off before they bloom,
And heaven nourishes with floods
Of hopeful tears, her second womb.

How many petals yet will fall
Before the aging stems are bare?
How many losses till the call
For us, my friend, to join her there?

But if you count them, though they sting
More than the babes of Bethlehem,
Mark this: As long as Christ is king,
My love will not be one of them.

HOW A GRANDMOTHER KNITS

She sits, the needles in her hands
looping and hooking her heart
into this little blue blanket,
and without any pink strands
stitches closed her wounds.

TAKE US TO YOURSELF TOGETHER

Woman, woman of my heart,
Woman of my flesh a part,
O I love you and with tears
Meditate upon the years
I might have to spend alone,
If our Father takes you home.
Could I stand such stormy weather?
O dear Father, test me not.
Such great strength is not my lot;
Take us to Yourself together.

BUT IF I DIE

She wrapped her husband in a shroud,
And then she knelt, kissed him, and vowed:
"I promise, since you can't remain,
Your death will not have been in vain."

✴ desiringGod

If you would like to further explore the vision of God and life presented in this book, we at Desiring God would love to serve you. We have hundreds of resources to help you grow in your passion for Jesus Christ and help you spread that passion to others. At our website, desiringGod.org, you'll find almost everything John Piper has written and preached, including more than thirty books. We've made over twenty-five years of his sermons available free online for you to read, listen to, download, and in some cases watch.

In addition, you can access hundreds of articles, find out where John Piper is speaking, learn about our conferences, discover our God-centered children's curricula, and browse our online store. John Piper receives no royalties from the books he writes and no compensation from Desiring God. The funds are all reinvested into our gospel-spreading efforts. Desiring God also has a whatever-you-can-afford policy, designed for individuals with limited discretionary funds. If you'd like more information about this policy, please contact us at the address or phone number below. We exist to help you treasure Jesus Christ and his gospel above all things because he is most glorified in you when you are most satisfied in him. Let us know how we can serve you!

Desiring God
Post Office Box 2901 Minneapolis, Minnesota 55402
888.346.4700   mail@desiringGod.org